YOUR KNOWLEDGE HAS VALUE

- We will publish your bachelor's and master's thesis, essays and papers

- Your own eBook and book - sold worldwide in all relevant shops

- Earn money with each sale

Upload your text at www.GRIN.com
and publish for free

Gitta Glüpker

Media and Terrorism

GRIN Verlag

Bibliografische Information der Deutschen Nationalbibliothek:

Die Deutsche Bibliothek verzeichnet diese Publikation in der Deutschen National-
bibliografie; detaillierte bibliografische Daten sind im Internet über http://dnb.d-
nb.de/ abrufbar.

Imprint:

Copyright © 2008 GRIN Verlag GmbH
Druck und Bindung: Books on Demand GmbH, Norderstedt Germany
ISBN: 978-3-640-31614-4

This book at GRIN:

http://www.grin.com/en/e-book/124570/media-and-terrorism

GRIN - Your knowledge has value

Der GRIN Verlag publiziert seit 1998 wissenschaftliche Arbeiten von Studenten, Hochschullehrern und anderen Akademikern als eBook und gedrucktes Buch. Die Verlagswebsite www.grin.com ist die ideale Plattform zur Veröffentlichung von Hausarbeiten, Abschlussarbeiten, wissenschaftlichen Aufsätzen, Dissertationen und Fachbüchern.

Visit us on the internet:

http://www.grin.com/

http://www.facebook.com/grincom

http://www.twitter.com/grin_com

Yeditepe University

Fall term 2008/2009

POLS 455 Terrorism in Context

Media and Terrorism

Istanbul, November 11th, 2008

Gitta Glüpker

Table of Contents

1. Introduction

As the lecture on "Terrorism in Context" has shown, terrorism is an extremely complex phenomenon which can involve a multitude of motives, strategies and actors. Even if terrorism is not an invention of the modern age but it has its roots in the ancient times, the contemporary forms of terrorism display special features. One of them is the *"media-oriented terrorism"* (Martin 2003: 281). It is linked to the emergence of mass media that allow a global and life coverage of terrorist acts.

This paper will examine which role the media play for terrorism. How do the media treat the phenomenom of terrorism (chapter 2)? After a brief summary of guidelines of news media the major focus will lie on the coverage of terrorist incidents in reality. As another feature of the media's perspective the governmental attempts to restrict the freedom of reporting will be described.

The second part of this paper will deal with the media's role for terrorist strategies (chapter 3). What does media-oriented terrorism mean concretely?

Chapter 5 draws a conclusion from the precedent analysis, after chapter 4 has dealt with the delicate: What are the effects of the media's involvement in terrorism?

Gus Martin's book "Understanding terrorism" served as the basic source for this paper because it offers a broad and detailed overview on the topic. It is striking that there seem to be no differences in opinion among experts on the relationship between media and terrorism: Other authors whose findings have also been considered for this work (see references) all share Martin's perception.

2.   The Media's Perspective

2.1   The Basics: Professional Standards and News Criteria

Most professionals in the media field agree on some basic standards that should be applied by journalists and editorial teams who are providing news (Martin 2003: 297). These standards are:

- *objectivity;*
- *fairness;* and
- *accuracy* regarding the research done before publishing the news.

Concerning the coverage of terrorist acts there are also some guidelines that most journalists would agree to, at least in theory:

a)   Journalists should neither serve as spokesmen/ spokeswomen for the terrorists nor should they publish sheer propaganda without showing challenging points of view as well.

b)   Reporting should not heroizate or romanticize terrorism.

c)   Journalists should hold back certain information if their publishing would represent an "immediate danger to life and limb" (Martin 2003: 297).

d)   Journalists should never try to become active themselves in the process of crisis solution; their job is to report on the process but not to influence them.

2.2   Reporting on Terrorism in Reality: Grey Zones and 'Painful Decisions'

As Paletz and Boiney say, media executives "face painful decisions when provided by terrorists with videos of hostages they have executed or of their captives making apparently voluntary but probably coerced statements" (Paletz and Boiney 1992: 8, see also El-Nawawy 2004).

The issue arises from the *conflict between the ideal professional standards* as shown in chapter 2.1 and the fact that media are strongly influenced by *market competition*:

Print-media, broadcasting stations and also internet news companies are corporations that *compete with others for market shares*. Hence, their product – the news – have to meet the desire of their clients, i. e. the audience. That is mostly the case when the news concern

- dramatic incidents;
- stories of individuals with a strong emotional aspect;
- stories that directly affect the audience; and
- stories with a 'negative quality' (Weichert 2005). (Martin 2003: 285/86)

This precondition for economic success leads to the need to produce news with *"exclusivity" status and "scoops"*: Journalists have to strive for stories that their competitors do not know yet so that they are the first to report. In this case one speaks of a "scoop". Or they try to get interviews or background information nobody else on the market possesses so that their information is exclusive. If these stories stay out journalists also use *"spinning"*, i. e. they stress a particular aspect of an incident that would normally not be newsworthy so that it suddenly turns into "news" and seems to be urgent. (Martin 2003: 291)

The pressure on journalists and the new technologies that speed up all communication processes produce a *'realtime reflex'* and a *'breaking news mentality'* among media professionals, as Weichert states. (both Weichert 2005).

Two examples should be described to illustrate the 'realtime reflex':

a)   *Al Qaeda videos on TV channels:* Journalists often do not have the time to reflect critically, neither on the content of the video messages not on ots effect on the terrorist environment. Furthermore, they can be sure that if they do not broadcast the video, some of their competitors certainly will do so. These factors lead to the sending of Al Qaeda videos on many TV channels. (Weichert 2005)

b)   *Kidnapping of tourists by Abu Sayyaf in 2000:* Abu Sayyaf ("Sword of God") is an islamic terrorist group operating in the Southern Philippines. In April 2000 a group of Abu Sayyaf fighters captured 20 tourists and staff from a hotel and took them to the jungle of the Filipino island of Jolo. The hostages were held there for weeks, some even for month. During that period, many journalists came to the island and followed the group's odyssee through the forest. They were offered to visit the camp and to interview the kidnappers – and they accepted the offer. Pictures of the suffering hostages were published on TV and in the printmedia. (Wikipedia 2008)

All in all, media give priority to terrorist incidents: On the one hand terrorism certainly is relevant for the political development so that it is the media's responsibility to keep the people informed. But it is even more important that terrorism offers a great potential for sensationalization.

A last feature of reporting on media is the *inconsistence in the choice of news, the reporting and the labelling of terrorists*. As well as the international community and experts, also "the world media systems have not agreed on a universal definition of terror" either (el-Nawawy 2004). Since labelling is highly subjective, it depends on the position of the reporter if he/ she pictures the terrorists as such or if they consider them as "freedom fighters".

Next to the broad scale of possible labels „the selection, depiction, and meaning of iconic images, and the choice of experts for commentary" (Norris, Kern and Just: 2003, see also el-Nawawy 2004) can lead to deviations from the ideal objectivity, too.

2.3   The limits of journalism: governmental regulation

In case of dissident terrorism, governments have to respond to their aggressors. They seek the public support for their policies if they do not want to risk the political and social balance of their state. Since public opinion is strongly influenced by mass media, the media spin (see chapter 2.2) is an *important factor for policy makers*. This is why most governments will try to influence the media's coverage, especially by controlling the media's access to governmental information. (Martin 2003: 280)

That *both sides, terrorists as well as governments, use the media* in order to spread 'their' pictures, was shown, for example, by the kidnapping of the Dubrovka theatre in Moskow by Chechen separatists in 2002.

The *freedom of press can be restricted to very different extends* (Martin 2003: 290):

If one analyses systems in which freedom of press is at least theoretically considered as an ideal standard, government and media are actors that are relatively independent from each other. Therefore, one has to consider two different ways of restriction:

a) *Gatekeeping:* This means the self-restriction of journalists, e. g. by codes of conduct. One example is the code of conduct by the British National Union of Journalists (NUJ 2006). Gatekeeping is usually aiming to obviate a restriction by the state. In the aftermath of September 11th, several institutions have called for special codes of conduct for the reporting on terrorism, e. g. the Council of Europe Parliamentary Assembly in 2005 (COE 2005). Since self-restriction can be quite fluid and inconsistent it still enables the media to sensationalize and spin their stories.

b) *Official regulation:* Governments limit the release of information, especially in wartimes; the legislation includes laws that allow the surpression of reporting on issues that are considered as crucial to national security. Furthermore, the state run or semi-state run media stick to the professional standards more closely than private media, also because they are not as exposed to the market pressure as private media are.

If even democratic regimes see the necessity to restrict the freedom of press in some cases it is not surprising that this practice can also be found in non-democratic regimes:

c) *State-regulated press in authoritarian regimes:* Private media enterprises exist but their news are censored and penalty laws are surpressing unfavorable reporting. (Martin 2003: 299)

d) *State-regulated press in totalitarian regimes:* There are no private media. The state controls all news. In such systems, terrorists cannot use the official media for their purposes at all. (Martin 2003: 299)

3. The Terrorist's Perspective

3.1 The Terrorist's Interest in the Media

Since terrorists follow the rationale "kill one, terrorize a thousand" (Martin 2003: 10) the media's attention to terrorist actions constitute the *crucial factor which makes the terrorist calculus work out* (Alexander 1979: 160). In fact, terrorists have three aims when it comes to the news coverage of their activity (Martin 2003: 289):

a) They want to inform the public about *their cause*. They need the independent mass media for this objective since state-run media will probably not report on them in a manner that serves their public image.

b) They want to transport *their message* (e. g. "our cause is just, and the ennemy's is unjust", Martin 2003: 59).

c) They want to influence the *public opinion* and consequently the governmental policies: the mass media coverage of a terrorist act "can lead to public pressure for the […] adversary" (Martin 2003: 282).

3.2 The Adaption to the Media's Criteria

Most terrorists understand that they have to adapt to the media's criteria for news. This especially concerns the

- *degree of violence* they use in their actions; and
- the choice of *symbolism* in their actions (e. g. the choice of targets, the language used in press releases etc.).

The more spectacular their actions are the more probable it becomes that their actions will be picked by the media.

Furthermore, the terrorists offer *easily accessible and understandable information* on their movements since they know about the 'breaking news mentality' (see chapter 2.2) of journalists. They organize press conferences, produce press releases, offer interviews and produce video and audio files. (Martin 2003: 291)

Moreover, terrorists pay attention to the *efficieny* and *timeliness* of their communication with the media (Martin 2003: 282). Their strategy is efficient when the information are transported in an ordered manner that can be understood immediately. Timeliness is important because the information has to reach the public when the issue, i. e. the incident, is still relevant.

Eventually, as already mentioned introductorily, a form of *"media-orientated terrorism"* (Martin 2003: 281) has evolved during the last decades. It can be observed when terrorist acts are primarily carried out in order to attract the media's attention.

Last but not least, a extreme option for terrorists to use the media has to be mentioned: the *enforcement of media coverage*. Alexander gives some examples on such incidents when terrorists asked for media coverage on their cause (by advertisements in newspapers etc.) in return for the release of hostages (Alexander 1979: 161/2).

3.3 Media Links and Channels

How get terrorists in contact with journalists?

Some groups establish *direct or indirect links to reporters*. Other organizations run *aboveground organizations* that maintain official relationships with the media.

Some terrorist groups also use the internet to send *direct messages* to the public by putting information on internet sites. (Martin 2003: 281 and Weichert 2004) This allows them to bypass the media companies. The disaadvantage is that it reaches only a limited audience.

It can be said that terrorists make use of all types of media formats:

a) *Print media* are certainly the oldest among the media channels used by terrorist groups. Since the 19th century private newspaper exist and technologies allow the easy production of critical publications. Terrorists maintain relationships to sympathetic publishers or run clandestine press.

b) *Radio broadcasting* is a way of disseminating propaganda that is used since the beginnings of the 20th century. Clandestine radio enables terrorists to reach many people, especially in areas that are without widespread use of TV.

c) *Television* is the most usedul tool to reach as many people as possible since most people have a television at home. It combines life and visiual messages with "on-the-scene audio" which reflects the entire drama of an terrorist incident.

d) The *Internet* is "extensively used by many terrorist groups" (Martin 2003: 281) because it allows the combination of text, audio and video files as well as an interactive relationship with the audience via mails, forums etc. Furthermore, it is the quickest channel of information and will keep the information accessible even long time after the incident occurred.

4.   The Effects of the Media's Involvement in Terrorism

On the one hand, the extensive coverage of terrorist acts by the media can be considered as the *fulfilment of the main purpose of the media*: to keep the public entirely informed. Also, in an ideal society the free press should show all aspects of terrorism so that *politically mature citizens* would be able to judge by themselves on what they see, read and hear. Under such circumstandes the coverage of terrorist movements and their actions would probably lead to "public hostility towards terrorists" (Barkan and Snowden 2000: 84). (Martin 2003: 292).

Unfortunately, such an ideal society does not exist. For the media's side this has it has been shown in chapter 2.2 and 2.3. Hence, on the other hand, there are some serious points of *criticism about journalists that cross the line* between sheer objective reporting and disseminating terrorist's propaganda:

a) It is an ***ethical problem*** when victims are humiliazed and their families and friends have to suffer additional pain because journalists publish detailed information and pictures on their suffering through terrorist attacks. (Weichert 2005)

b) When journalists cover only the obvious incidents without offering a well-reflected analysis of its background (due to economic and time contraints, see chapter 2.2) the risk of ***misunderstandings and misinterpretations*** by the public occur.

c) When journalists barge in the process of anti-terror-measures or conflict resolution they might ***complicate the efforts to end terrorism.*** (Alexander 1979: 164/65) As a consequence of the need for exclusive information (see chapter 2.2) journalists have

- interfered in on-going operations;
- increased the pressure on governmental agencies to take publicly noticeable measures against the terrorists (even these were not as effective as hidden measures);
- put pressure on terrorist participants, especially former hostages, to give interviews;
- delivered with their reporting intelligence information to the terrorists that endangered lifes additionally;
- in interviews pushed terrorists to strenghten their demands towards the adversary, e. g. with the question whether the terrorists had set a deadline during a hijacking. Even if the terrorists might have not thought of such a deadline before, the question 'inspired' them to set one.

d) Reporting on terrorist incidents and its consequences can ***encourage terrorists and its supporters*** to stick to their strategy. Furthermore, the information can serve as an input for later actions because they might reveal "weaknesses" and help to improve the terrorist's plans.

e) The news on terrorist motivations and actions might raise the sympathy of onlookers and analysts, i. e. ***manipulate the political environment***. This can weaken the main target of the terrorists. Firstly, the ***domestic pressure*** might grow to soften the governmental stance towards the terrorists. Secondly, also ***international pressure*** on the government might develop due to media coverage on the conflict. Eventually, this is the achievement that terrorists seek for: their actions raised the attention of the public and this indirect pressure forces the other side to surrender.

f) As Martin says, also the "theoretical influence of media exposure on the future behaviour of other like-minded extremists" (Martin 2003: 295), the so-called ***contagion effect***, has to be considered: Especially in times of New Terrorism, that is characterized by independent cells striving for the same goal (e. g. Al Qaeda) and by modern communication technologies, *learning processes run fast*. Successful terrorist attacks can motivate other cells to repeat the plan and terrorist incidents might occur more and more often. (see also Alexander 1979: 163)

Apart from these negative effects the past has shown that some positive outcomes of media coverage are possible nonetheless: Firstly, under certain conditions, an unfavorable effect for the terrorists can occur - *the backlash*. This happens especially if the terrorist's adversary also possesses a successful communication strategy towards the media. In such a case, the reporting on terrorist attacks will strengthen the public support for the government and weaken the terrorist's position in the public opinion. Secondly, the reporting on on-going terrorist incidents can also reduce the pressure on terrorists because of their *"ventilating" effect* (Alexander 1979: 166). Eventually, this can save lifes.

5. Conclusion

"The media are the terrorist's best friend" - this assessment made by Alexander almost 30 years ago (Alexander 1979: 160) still holds true, even more than ever in the times of modern communication technologies. As this paper has shown, both sides need each other: the terrorist calculus is based on the public attention. To an increasing extend, mass media use terrorist incidents to fulfil the expectations of their audience and to successfully compete with the others.

The interference of media and terrorism in the business of the respective other side can have positive side-effects. Still, it has become more than obvious that the negative outcomes outweigh the public benefit of media coverage on terrorism.

Especially in democratic countries where the principle of free press is taken seriously, *solutions to this dilemma are difficult* to push through. It seems that the only realistic approaches are the journalistic self-regulation or a moderate regulation by governments. The root of the problem probably will never disappear: the human interest in the tragedies of others.

6.   References

Alexander, Y.(1979): *Terrorism and the Media: Some Considerations. In Terrorism. Theory and Pracice.* (Ed. Alexander, Y., Carlton, D. and Wilkinson, P.). Boulder: Westview Press.

Barkan, S. E., and Snowden L. (2000). *Collective Violence.* Boston: Allyn & Bacon.

Council of Europe (COE) (20 June 2005): *Media coverage of terrorist acts: PACE calls for a code of conduct for journalists.* COE: https://wcd.coe.int/ViewDoc.jsp?id=874599 &Site=DC&BackColorInternet=DBDCF2&BackColorIntranet=FDC864&BackColorL ogged=FDC864, last access 10 November 2008.

El-Nawawy, M. (2004). *Terrorist or Freedom Fighter?: The Arab Media Coverage of "Terrorism" or "So-Called Terrorism".* Global Media Journal, Volume 3, Issue 5, Fall 2004.

Martin, G. (2003). *Understanding Terrorism.* Thousand Oaks: Sage Publications.

National Union of Journalists (NUJ) (20 June 2006): *Code of Conduct.* NUJ: http://media.gn.apc.org/nujcode.html, last access 10 November 2008.

Norris, P. Kern, M. and Just, M. (2003). *Framing terrorism. In Framing terrorism: The news media, the government, and the public.* (Ed. Norris, P., Kern, M. and Just. M.). New York: Routledge.

Paletz, D. and Boiney, J. (1992). *Researchers' perspectives. In Terrorism and the media.* (Ed. Paletz, D. and Schmid, A.). London: SAGE Publications.

Weicher, S. A. (21 June 2004): *Zwischen Sensationslust und Chronistenpflicht.* [Between sensational mongering and the duty as a chronicler.] Medienheft: http://www.medien heft.ch/kritik/bibliothek/k22_WeichertStephanAlexander.html, 21.06.2004, last access 28.10.2008.

Weichert, S. A. (25 January 2005): *Der terroristisch-mediale Beziehungskomplex.* [The complex relation between Terrorism and Media.] Telepolis: http://www.heise.de/ tp/r4/artikel/19/19291/1.html, last access 05 November 2008.

Wikipedia (3 October 2008): *Entführungsfall Aby Sayaf.* [Abu Sayaf's case of kidnapping.] http://de.wikipedia.org/wiki/Wallert, last access 05 November 2008.